Cool STUFF —for—

READING & WRITING

A Division of ABDO
ABDO
Publishing Company

PAM SCHEUNEMANN

visit us at www.abdopublishing.com

Published by ABDO Publishing Company, a division of ABDO, P.O. Box 398166, Minneapolis, Minnesota 55439. Copyright © 2012 by Abdo Consulting Group, Inc. International copyrights reserved in all countries. No part of this book may be reproduced in any form without written permission from the publisher. Checkerboard Library™ is a trademark and logo of ABDO Publishing Company.

Printed in the United States of America, North Mankato, Minnesota
052011
092011

♻ PRINTED ON RECYCLED PAPER

Design and Production: Mighty Media, Inc.
Series Editors: Katherine Hengel and Liz Salzmann
Photo Credits: Anders Hanson, Shutterstock

The following manufacturers/names appearing in this book are trademarks:
3M™ Scotch®, Bic® Round Stic™, DMC®, Mead®, Rubber Stampede™, Sharpie®, Tombow® Mono Adhesive™, VersaColor™

Library of Congress Cataloging-in-Publication Data
Scheunemann, Pam, 1955-
  Cool stuff for reading & writing : creative handmade projects for kids / Pam Scheunemann.
    p. cm. -- (Cool stuff)
  Includes index.
  ISBN 978-1-61714-982-5
  1. Language arts (Elementary) 2. Creative activities and seat work--Juvenile literature. 3. Language experience approach in education. 4. Education, Elementary--Activity programs. I. Title. II. Title: Cool stuff for reading and writing.
  LB1576.S324 2011
  372.6'044--dc22
                          2011003500

CONTENTS

THE FINE ART OF

READING &

People have been reading and writing since ancient times. Today we can communicate using text messages, e-mails, and electronic books. But many people still enjoy writing on paper and reading printed books.

In this book you'll find some fun ways to enhance your reading and writing experiences. You could make your own book covers, bookplates, and bookmarks. You could also decorate a special pen or notepad.

So get ready to learn how to create your own sense of reading and writing style!

WRITING

Permission & Safety

- Always get **permission** before making any type of craft at home.
- Ask if you can use the tools and supplies needed.
- If you'd like to do something by yourself, say so. Just make sure you do it safely.
- Ask for help when necessary.
- Be careful when using knives, scissors, or other sharp objects.

Be Prepared

- Read the entire activity before you begin.
- Make sure you have all the tools and **materials** listed.
- Do you have enough time to complete the project?
- Keep your work area clean and organized.
- Follow the directions for each activity.
- Clean up after you are finished for the day.

TOOLS AND

CIRCLE PUNCH

BIC ROUND STIC PENS

FELT

PADDING COMPOUND

STRAIGHT PINS

GREEN FLORIST TAPE

DOUBLE-SIDED TAPE

MONO ADHESIVE

EMBROIDERY NEEDLES

HOLE PUNCH

BINDER CLIPS

MICROBEADS

MATERIALS

PLAIN BRICK

WIRE CUTTERS

**SILK FLOWER
WITH STEM**

THIN CORDING

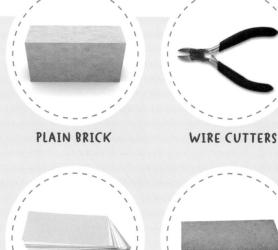

CARDSTOCK

CHIPBOARD

SPIRAL NOTEBOOK

EMBROIDERY FLOSS

PONY BEADS

INK PADS

CRAFT PAINT

RUBBER STAMPS

Decorated
POSH PENS

THESE BEAUTIES WILL PUT REGULAR PENS TO SHAME!

STUFF YOU'LL NEED

SILK FLOWER WITH STEM DOUBLE-SIDED TAPE RULER
WIRE CUTTERS MICROBEADS PONY BEADS
BIC ROUND STIC PENS PAPER PLATE SCISSORS
GREEN FLORIST TAPE EMBROIDERY FLOSS

FLOWER PEN

1. If possible, push the leaves up by the silk flower. Remove any leaves lower on the stem. Cut the stem to about 2½ inches (6 cm) long. You may need wire cutters to cut through it.

2. Using the green florist tape, begin wrapping the pen. Start at the black part of the pen by the tip. Wrap only about halfway up the pen. Be sure to **overlap** the tape and smooth any wrinkles.

3. When you get halfway up the pen, add the flower. Hold the flower in place while you wrap the tape around the stem and the pen. Wrap it tightly so the flower will stay in place.

BEADED PEN

1. Wrap the white barrel of the pen with double-sided tape.

2. Remove the backing. Try not to touch the tape too much. The oil from your fingers makes it less sticky.

3. Pour the microbeads onto a paper plate.

4. Roll the pen in the beads. Be sure to cover the pen completely.

5. Roll the beaded pen in your hands to secure the beads.

TIP

Put some rice or dried beans in the bottom of a pot, jar, or glass to hold your pens.

FLOSS PEN

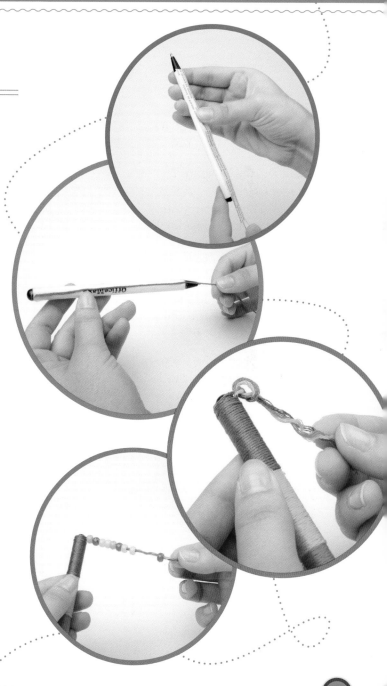

1. Wrap the white barrel of the pen with double-sided tape. Remove the backing.

2. Choose four colors of floss to wrap your pen with. Set one end of the first color of floss lengthwise on the pen.

3. Wrap the floss tightly around the pen, starting at the edge of the barrel. Wrap one-fourth of the pen. Cut the floss and press the end firmly to the tape.

4. Start wrapping the second color at the end of the first color. Wrap one-fourth of the pen. Then run the floss straight along the pen to the top. Leave about 4 inches (10 cm) of floss hanging off the end of the pen.

5. Repeat step 4 with the third and fourth colors of floss. The pen should now be completely covered.

6. Tie the three colors of floss together. Make the knot as close to the end of the pen as possible.

7. Add about 1½ inches (4 cm) of pony beads. Tie a big knot at the end. Make sure the beads can't fit over the knot.

Nifty
NOTEPADS

WRITE YOUR NOTES IN STYLE!

STUFF YOU'LL NEED

STACK OF PAPER
CARDSTOCK
CHIPBOARD
BINDER CLIPS
PADDING COMPOUND

FOAM BRUSH
SPIRAL NOTEBOOK
RULER
DECORATIVE PAPER
PENCIL

HOLE PUNCH
SCISSORS
MONO ADHESIVE
DECORATIONS

MAKE YOUR OWN NOTEPAD

1 Gather a **stack** of paper. The sheets should all be the same size. You can use any number of sheets.

2 Cut a piece of cardstock the same size as the paper. Put it on top of the stack for the cover. Cut a piece of chipboard the same size as the paper. Put it under the stack for the back cover of the pad.

3 Cut two pieces of white paper the same size as your pad. Put one on each side of the pad. This will protect the covers from drips.

4 Tap the stack on the table until all the edges on one side are even. Be sure to include the covers and the inside sheets of paper.

5 Put a binder clip on each side to hold the paper tightly together. Turn up the side you tapped on the table. Brush it with padding compound. Let it dry a few minutes. Add a second coat of padding compound. Let it dry completely.

6 Remove the binder clips and white paper. Decorate the cover any way you like.

DECORATE A NOTEPAD

1   Measure the length and width of the **spiral** notebook. Include the area where the spiral binding is. Cut a piece of white paper to that exact size. This will be the **template**.

2   Cut a piece of decorative paper to the same size. Cut two pieces if you want to cover both the front and back of the pad.

(3) Round the corners on one side to match the corners of the bottom of the notebook.

(4) Line up the template with the notebook cover. Using a pencil, make a circle for each of the spiral holes.

(5) Punch holes on the template where the circles are.

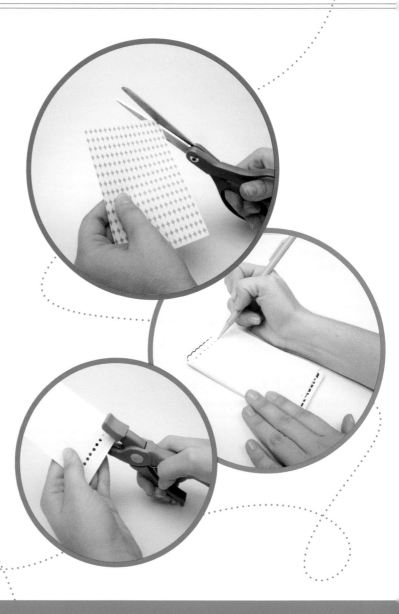

(6) Place the **template** on the decorative paper. Use the template as a guide for punching the holes in the decorative paper.

(7) Use a scissors to cut from the edge of the decorative paper to each hole.

(8) Put the decorative paper on the notebook. Position the holes over the **spiral** binding. Press the paper into the gaps. Make sure it fits the cover nicely.

(9) Lift the decorative paper and put Mono Adhesive on the notebook cover. Lower the decorative paper and press firmly. Keep the edges of the decorative paper even with the notebook cover.

10 Decorate the notebook any way you like!

TIP

Sharpen the hole punch by punching aluminum foil.

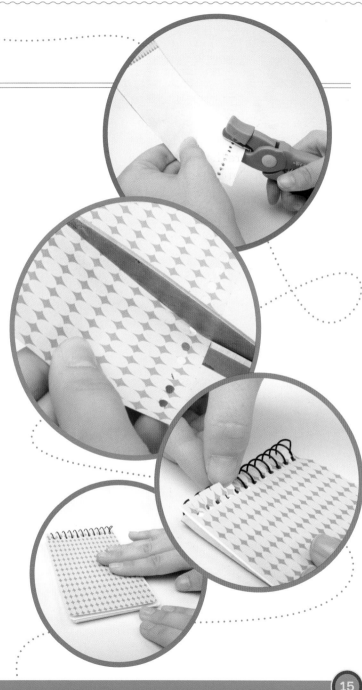

BOOKMARKS

YOU'LL ALWAYS FIND YOUR PLACE!

STUFF YOU'LL NEED

- LARGE PAPER CLIPS
- THIN CORD
- RULER
- SCISSORS
- BEADS

- THIN RIBBON
- CARDSTOCK
- TAPE
- MARKERS & STICKERS
- DECORATIVE PAPER

- 1-INCH CIRCLE PUNCH
- SMALL PHOTOS
- MONO ADHESIVE

BEAD PAGE CLIPS

1   Cut a piece of thin cord about 10 inches (25 cm) long. Tie it to a large paper clip.

2   Put on the beads. Leave about 2 inches (5 cm) of cord at the end.

3   Tie a double knot in the end of the cord. Trim any extra cord.

RIBBON PAGE CLIPS

1   Cut several pieces of ribbon 12 inches (30.5 cm) long. Fold a ribbon in half. Put the loop through the end of a paper clip.

2   Pull both ends of the ribbon through the loop. Pull tight.

3   Repeat steps 1 and 2 with the other ribbons.

CLASSY CORNER
BOOKMARKS

1. Cut a piece of cardstock 4 × 8½ inches (10 × 21 cm).

2. Fold two corners of the cardstock to the center.

3. Close the **seam** with tape or a sticker.

4. Decorate the front with your name or stickers.

TIP

*Make a smaller **version** of this bookmark by using a smaller piece of cardstock. Fold the corners to meet in the center. Trim any extra cardstock off the bottom to make a triangle.*

FANCY PHOTO BOOKMARKS

1   Cut a strip of decorative paper 2 × 11 inches (5 × 28 cm). Fold it in half lengthwise.

2   On one half, use the circle punch to make holes for the photos. You can fit up to three photo circles.

3   Cut out the photos. Make sure the photos are at least as big as the holes, but smaller than the bookmark.

4   Put Mono Adhesive around the holes on the back side. Get right up to the edges of the holes. Press the photos into place.

5   Put Mono Adhesive on the inside of the other half. Be sure to get right up to the edges.

6   Starting at the fold, press the two halves together.

TIP

To make a nice fold, match up the bottom edges. Hold the edges together and press away from the fold. Smooth by rubbing the handle of a scissors across the fold.

BOOKPLATES

STUFF YOU'LL NEED

PAPER
SCISSORS
PENCIL
RUBBER STAMPS

INK PAD
MARKERS
STICKERS
MONO ADHESIVE

1   Cut pieces of paper to the size you want your bookplates to be. Don't make them too big. They need to fit inside small books too.

2   Do some **sketches** with paper and pencil to **design** your bookplate.

3   Copy your design onto your bookplate sheets. Use markers, rubber stamps, and stickers. Let the ink dry completely.

4   Use Mono Adhesive to glue the bookplates to the inside front covers of your books.

TIP

Many bookplates say Ex Libris *on them. It means "from the books of" in Latin. You can write it in English. Write "From the books of" or "From the library of" before your name on your bookplates.*

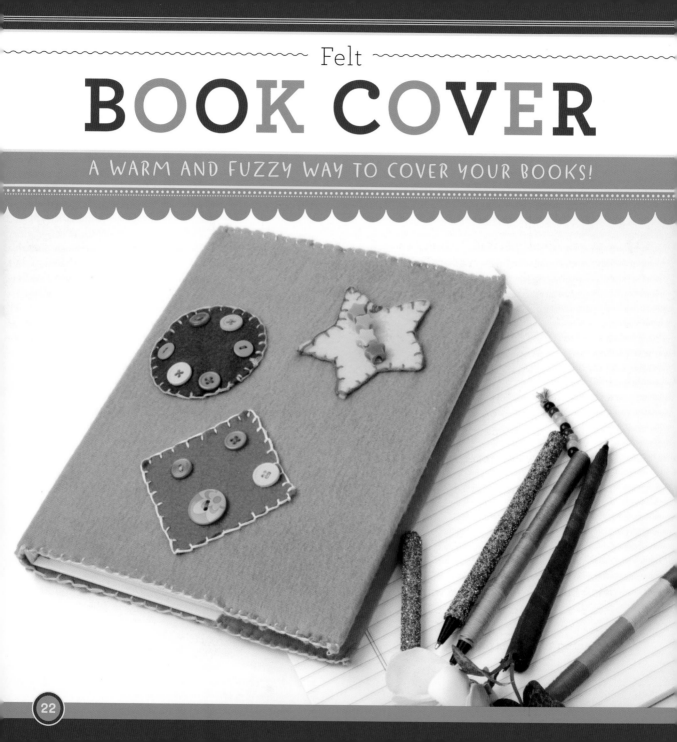

BOOK COVER

A WARM AND FUZZY WAY TO COVER YOUR BOOKS!

STUFF YOU'LL NEED

BOOK	FELT (SEVERAL COLORS)	BEADS
NEWSPAPER	STRAIGHT PINS	BUTTONS
PENCIL	EMBROIDERY NEEDLE	PAPER
SCISSORS	EMBROIDERY FLOSS	RULER

1. Open the book you want to cover and lay it on a sheet of newspaper. Trace around the book. Be sure the spine is flat as you trace around each side. This makes sure you'll have enough **felt** to cover the book when it is closed.

2. Add an extra 3 inches (7 cm) to each side for the book flaps. Add an extra ¼ inch (.6 cm) to the top and bottom. Cut out the newspaper pattern.

3. Now you know how much felt you need. Buy a large piece for the book cover. Get small pieces of other colors for decorating.

4. Place the newspaper pattern on the large piece of felt. Line a corner of the pattern up with a corner of the felt. This will keep you from wasting felt. Pin the pattern to the felt. Put several pins along each side. Cut the felt along the edges of the pattern.

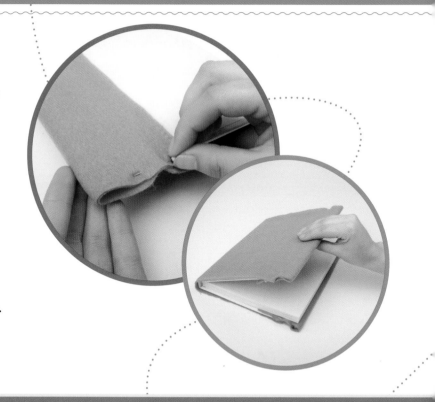

5   Unpin the pattern. Lay the book open in the center of the **felt**. Fold 3 inches (7 cm) around the front cover.

6   Pin the edges of the felt together at the top and bottom.

7   Do the same thing on the back cover. Close the book to make sure the cover is the right size. It should fit **snugly** around the book. **Adjust** the flaps if needed, but keep them the same size.

USING EMBROIDERY FLOSS

*Embroidery floss comes in many beautiful colors. There are six **strands** of thread in each piece of floss. The strands must be separated for most projects that require embroidery floss.*

*The blanket **stitch** used in this project calls for three strands. Cut a piece of floss about 2 feet (61 cm) long. Pinch the end of the floss between two fingers. Separate the strands. Grasp one strand and gently pull it away from the others. Repeat until you have three strands. Put the ends of the strands together and thread them through the needle.*

8. Draw some pencil **sketches** of the cover **design** you want. Will you layer **felt** pieces? Will you add beads or buttons?

9. If you plan to add felt shapes, draw the shapes on paper. Cut them out to use as patterns.

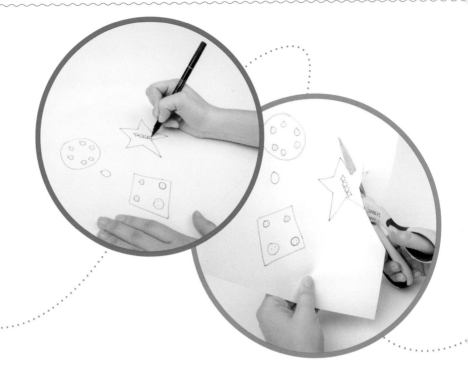

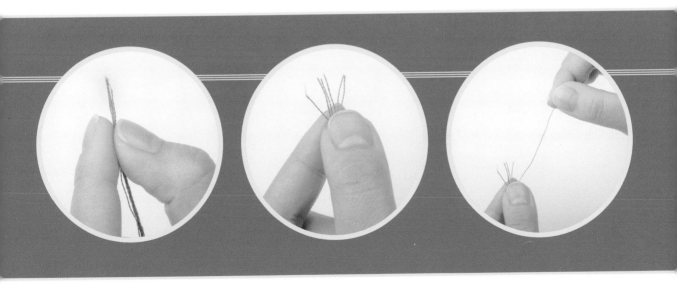

10. Pin the pattern to the color of **felt** you want to use. Cut it out.

11. Sew beads or buttons to the shapes before adding them to the book cover.

12. Put the shapes on the book cover where you want them. Pin them in place.

13. Use the blanket **stitch** to sew the shapes onto the book cover.

14. Use the blanket stitch to sew along the top of the book cover. Start at one side, sewing the flap to the felt cover. Then continue to stitch the felt across the top of the book. When you get to the other flap, sew it to the felt cover as well.

15. Repeat step 14 on the bottom of the felt cover.

HOW TO DO THE BLANKET STITCH

The blanket **stitch** is an embroidery stitch that looks nice on both sides. It is often used for the edges of a project, such as a blanket! You can use thread the same color as your **felt**. Or choose a different color that will show against the felt.

1   Separate out three **strands** of floss (See page 24).

2   Thread the strands through the needle. Pull it down a bit so it doesn't go back out of the needle. Tie a knot in the longer end.

3   Position the needle behind the felt about ¼ inch (.6 cm) from the edge.

4   Push the needle up through the felt from the back to the front. Pull it until the knot hits the back of the felt.

5   Move the needle about ¼ inch (.6 cm) to the right of where the thread came up. Push the needle up through the felt again.

6   Pull the floss through most of the way. Leave a little loop.

7   Put the needle through the loop from left to right. Pull it **snug**.

8   Repeat steps 5 through 7.

9   When you reach the end of the thread or the end of the felt, you'll need to make a knot. Push the needle through the top of the last stitch. Before pulling it all the way, put it through the loop you just made. Pull tight to make a knot.

10   To hide the end, run the needle from the edge of the felt in about ¼ inch (.6 cm). Pull it through. Cut the thread off right next to the felt.

STUFF YOU'LL NEED

PLAIN BRICKS
CRAFT PAINT
PAINTBRUSH
STICKERS

MARKERS
GEMS
FELT
PAPER

PENCIL
SCISSORS
STRAIGHT PINS
GLUE

1   Paint two bricks with a background color. Let them dry.

2   Decorate the bricks using paint, markers, stickers, or gems. Leave one side and one end undecorated.

3   Set the undecorated side on a piece of paper. Trace around the brick. Cut it out inside the lines to make a pattern.

4   Pin the paper pattern to the **felt**. Cut out the shape and unpin the pattern. Repeat this step to cut a second felt shape.

5   Place the felt shapes against the undecorated sides of the bricks. Trim off any edges that are sticking out.

6   Glue the felt to the undecorated sides of the bricks. Lay the bricks felt-side down while the glue dries.

CONCLUSION

It's important to take good care of your books. And you can have fun in the process. Make some of the projects in this book. You might find that reading and writing have just become a lot more interesting. Do some **research** on different things you can make to give your reading and writing more style. There's no end to the **variety** of things you can make out of what you have at home! With your new writing stuff you'll be ready to become a writer yourself!

Go a step further. Take some time to learn about the history of reading and writing. You'll be surprised at the things people used to write with and write on! You may even find some ideas for your very own projects.

GLOSSARY

adjust – to change something slightly to produce a desired result.

design – 1. to plan how something will appear or work. 2. the appearance or style of something.

felt – a soft, thick fabric.

material – something that other things can be made of, such as fabric, plastic, or metal.

overlap – to lie partly on top of something.

permission – when a person in charge says it's okay to do something.

research – the act of finding out more about something.

seam – the line where two edges meet.

sketch – a drawing.

snug – very tight or close-fitting.

spiral – a type of binding made of coiled wire or plastic.

stack – a pile of things placed one on top of the other.

stitch – a small length of thread left in fabric by moving the needle in and out one time.

strand – one of the threads or strings that make up a rope or cord.

template – a shape you draw or cut around to copy it onto something else.

variety – a collection of different types of one thing. An assortment.

version – a different form or type from the original.

Web Sites

INDEX